AF271415

100 things
not to say a (young)
widow*

(or widower)

by K.

a.k.a. The Cynical Widow

I would like to dedicate this book to all the strangers in the internet's various widow groups who helped me with advice, encouragement or just some kind words in those frequent moments when I questioned my sanity and my ability to go on.

The Author's note

Hi,

I'm K.

I'd like to start my note with briefly telling you about my story and how it led me to write this book.

I joined this horrible club on a sunny Saturday morning in September 2019. I got up, and the house was way too quiet. Then I found him. The moment of realization that he is gone is hands down the most horrific moment of my life. I was thirty-two and six months pregnant with our first.

The next few months were incredibly intense because the bureaucracy people have to fight does not care about your heartbreak or that you can barely function. I wanted to break down, but I didn't have the time or the option to do so. I still don't have it.

I had a newborn soon to take care of, and she has made every struggle worth it ever since. Then again, her love for her father, whom she never even met, breaks my heart every day – they are so alike and would have had so much fun and joy together.

I was fortunate that I could just stay at home with her for a year, and to be frank with you, the lockdowns and the fact that I didn't need to face people during that period in the first year were beneficial for my healing.

But then the world started to open up – I started to open up, go back to work and interact with people again.

Then, the comments started to come.

The ignorant ones, the nosy ones, and the facepalm ones. I consider myself quite lucky because, other than a few, I rarely received any rude or offensive comments or questions regarding me being a widow. The repetitiveness, however, made me react to these with an increasingly cynical attitude.

The unfortunate fact is that death, in general, is considered a taboo topic for many people. Consequently, when someone drops the 'widow bomb' on them, they often don't know what to say – but they feel like they should say *something*.

More often than not, this *something* is a question or comment that widows and widowers don't need to hear or do not want to answer.

I get it. It's hard – it's even hard to say something if you've experienced loss before. From my own experience, nine times out of ten, these questions and comments don't come from a negative or judgmental place – they are genuine and said with good intentions. But guess what?

The road to hell is paved with good intentions.

The second main characteristic of all these things is ignorance. And I get that, too. Widowhood is one of those things that unless someone has experienced it, they don't know. Just don't pretend to know.

The idea for this book was born from the comment, *"But you're too young to be a widow"*. About seventy-five percent of people reacted with this after they learned that I'm a widow. Then it got me thinking. What else do I hear often? What else do I read often in the groups and discussions I'm part of that often upset or trigger widows

– or make them to roll their eyes so hard it counts as a workout? And so, first, the list was born, then the book itself.

When reading these, at some (hopefully), you will exclaim in disbelief that someone actually said that, but there is not one made-up comment or question listed in this book. There might be similar ones that can look like duplicates or the same comment from two different perspectives. This was intentional.

As a disclaimer, I would like you to know that I am in no way a professional therapist or counselor. I'm just a regular person who experienced one of the hardest things ever to experience, and I am over all the inappropriate questions.

You may find some of my comments under the page titles cynical or even inappropriate – and that's okay. I admit some are borderline too far, but I think every author should be true to themselves. These comments are unapologetically me, and you should in no way take them seriously.

I would also like to highlight that, for the sake of practicality, I will use the word 'widow', but I mean both widows and widowers, male/female/non-binary, whether they were married or not. So, in this book, a widow = a person who lost their partner.

Hopefully, you will be better informed when speaking to a widow the next time. I would also like to acknowledge that there is no blanket rule or that will apply for all widows of the world. We are different people in different situations that are all unique; therefore, I tried to keep this book as general as possible or include scenarios that while not relevant to me, personally – could be relevant to others. I would also like to mention that I took my own situation as a base. Consequently, most of my observations and recommendations are to speak to widows who had a loving relationship with their deceased partner. There are other instances when the death of someone can even come as a relief or true freedom – but I can't speak for them because I was lucky enough to be loved until the end.

After reading this book, you might feel that you can't even say anything at all to a widow without risking being rude, hurtful, or triggering. That's not true. You just have to understand that the reaction to your words could be very different from the intent you had when saying them. I can also assure you that you do not have to comment or ask questions just for the sake of it. Those are the comments and questions that ended up in this book. A widow's grief journey shouldn't be interfered with by unsolicited commentary and nosy questions.

Be mindful, open, and understanding. It's only awkward if you make it to be.

I.

Clichés

(and things you say to make *yourself* feel better.)

1. YOU'RE SO STRONG/BRAVE/ETC...

Well, you didn't see me half an hour ago in the parking lot.

They are strong because that's their only option. Do you think they have the luxury of being able to fall apart, especially if they have kids? If you guessed no, then you are 1000% correct.

You don't see them cry. They go to work, kids are at school, and they are functioning? It's all a well curated façade. Just because they don't show it to the world, doesn't mean they don't suffer, often in silence, crying under the shower or into their pillows at night.

If you're close to the person, you can always just be there for them if and when needed. You wouldn't believe how many friendships end when someone loses their partner because people feel awkward around them. Therefore, avoid the widow in times when they need their circle the most. If you can, send them a care package. If it's not in your budget, send them a text. Their loss is only awkward for you if you make it that way. They will open up in time.

And if you're not close to them, don't expect them to share how they truly feel without letting the whole world see them at their most vulnerable.

2. "I KNOW HOW YOU FEEL"

No, you do not.
You can't. Even. Fathom it.

This usually comes when someone wants to show empathy, and that they feel for the person and their loss. But you don't know how they feel. Sure, you can have an educated guess, but even your best guess will be nothing compared to the crazy amount of emotions a widow feels in any given moment – especially at the beginning.

The most common polite answer for this usually comes in the form of an awkward smile, maybe accompanied by nodding. Someone may even tell you that no, you don't, possibly along with telling them how lucky they are that they don't know.

If you really want to help, you can say:
How are you feeling? Just know I am here for you if you'd like to talk.

If they don't want to, don't force it. They're not ready. And if they do, that's great. Make sure you're wearing your listening ears. But please, please, only offer if you are genuinely interested in how they feel. If you can listen without judgement. All you have to do is to validate their feelings (except self-guilt, shut that horrible nasty thing down in its roots).

3. EVERYTHING HAPPENS FOR A REASON

Sure. And the reason for this is that life is a [female dog].

This is one of the most common "comforting" lines, but that doesn't make it a good one. Seriously, never say this. Ever. It is awful, because no, there is no reason.

There are causes, of course, like a drunk driver or that we are still unable to cure all cancers, but what could be the reason for this happening right with them? That the universe hates them?

Come on.

~~Sometimes,~~ often, things just happen for no reason at all, especially bad things, especially with good people. We can't explain everything, nor should we try to.

4. HE / SHE IS IN A BETTER PLACE

You must think horrible of me as a wife if you consider six feet under a better place.

Look, I know. I know. Like with the last comment (and many others in the coming pages), you meant well.

Yes, we live in a terrible world; global warming and financial crises are always around the corner, the ice is melting, and the polar bears are going extinct. They are not lovely prospects, but I can assure you with the utmost certainty that they would want to be in this world with the widow. If this comment is accompanied by some religious seasoning, it's even worse, but we get to that on some later pages.

Instead of trying to convince them that their spouse is happier dead than alive, focus on the person, and make sure that they are in the right place. Widowhood can be very isolating; they've just lost the person they belonged together with, and unfortunately, most people who promise to be there for them – won't. Often, even long-time friends disappear because they feel awkward around the widow.

Just be there, and don't be upset if you are not thanked or appreciated right away. They will remember forever who was there for them and who was not.

5. YOU'RE TAKING IT SO WELL

You really believe that? In this case,
I would like to thank this award to the Academy, …

I can assure you, they are not taking it well.

Just because you can't see the tears, the struggles, the anxiety, and the distress, that doesn't mean they are not there. It just means that the person tries very hard to keep at least a fraction of their dignity. To carry their sorrow with their head held high up. The whole world doesn't have to see it – you don't have to see it.

Even if involuntarily, people pity widows, and they don't need anyone's pity.

Quite often, they don't even share how bad they feel with their closest family or friends. They just pretend that they are okay. They know they can't help, and they don't want to sadden them with their feelings or make them worry about them even more.

Instead of this, you can compliment them on how they're doing. Tell them that the funeral they organized was so nicely done. Reassure them when they doubt themselves. Hold them when they are about to fall.

6. AT LEAST THEY'RE NOT SUFFERING ANYMORE

Damn it.

You mean well. (I'm repeating myself, I know.) Guess what? They know.

If someone's partner passes after a battle with an illness or injury, they are fully aware of all the suffering they went through, and this is their tiny piece of silver lining.

And yes, of course, they are somewhat relieved that their loved one doesn't suffer anymore! But in their hopes, dreams, and prayers, the suffering ended with recovery and a happily ever after.

You don't have to point out the obvious. Instead, you can assure them how much their care helped and care for *them*. Pamper them (without smothering).

Caring for someone, especially if you know that you are likely to lose them, is a difficult and draining task. Being strong for them and for the kids, if there are any, they just go and go and go like a steam engine. And once it's over, the void is just too much. And I guarantee that they will keep powering through, and in the meantime they will need someone who will take care of them.

Be that someone. They will appreciate actions far more than words.

7. HE/SHE IS WITH GOD NOW

If he will now start supervising my guardian angel,
poor fella will quit.

It's very similar to the "he is in a better place" statement but trickier. It all depends on how religious the person is. But for the love of God, please don't say this to people who are not believers or not practicing religion.

I know some people who have found their faith after being widowed. Some others, who've lost theirs. And even if they are religious and actively practicing it, this comment is still not very comforting. I mean, they are with God, great, but they should be here. With them. That would be much, much better.

By the way, the same goes for: *"Now you have your own angel in heaven."*

They would prefer the deceased here on Earth, so not much of an ease either – their person is still in a place where they can't reach them, touch them, hug them, or kiss them.

The only possible comfort with these comments for anyone, is that imagining them in heaven is a nicer though than a wooden box underground or an urn on the fire mantle.

8. GOD WORKS IN MYSTERIOUS WAYS

He should focus on the starving children and work on THAT.

Staying with the religious comments, here is another one that has zero to no chance of being comforting to anyone. I firmly believe that this saying was born because even the most knowledgeable theologists could not make any sense of all the suffering and injustice in the world and explain why God would allow them to happen.

Sure, I presume you'd say this to swift any blame away from them and offer comfort in the idea that this was to happen due to fate or whatever out-of-this-world, higher power's decision.

From a widow's point of view, though, it's hardly comforting that they suffered this tremendous loss because the man in the sky is playing some deity version of Sims.

The question every widow will ask themselves, the universe, God (if they believe), and possibly everyone they know is: Why? If you provide this sentence as reasoning, you might as well have just thrown your arms in the air and shouted *just because*.

9. When my dad/mum/uncle/etc. died

My dad/mum/uncle/etc.. are fine, but now
I can't stop thinking what if something happens with them, too,
so thanks a lot.

You bring this up because that's the loss you've experienced, and you want to sympathize with the widow. While your loss and grief are valid, and no one doubts your feelings, respectfully, it's like comparing apples and pears.

Losing a grandparent or a parent is hard, but it's part of life. We know it's something we will need to face sooner or – hopefully – later in life. On the other hand, we don't expect to lose our significant other – or at least we imagine we will only lose them after growing old together.

Losing a partner is more than losing a person. It's losing the future that would have been lived, the years that should have been spent together. All the plans, hopes, and dreams they had – just gone. Losing a partner is losing a part of yourself.

All losses are devastating in their own different ways. If you went through grief, you can use your experience to help without feeling the need to compare them.

10. I CAN'T IMAGINE WHAT WOULD I DO IF THIS HAPPENED TO ME

Then don't imagine it. Or you know what, do. Maybe that will make you a little more compassionate and understanding.

When we encounter a tragedy, a sad event or life story, the thought of "What if this would be me" subconsciously goes through our mind. You don't need to say it out loud, though. Because while you can't even imagine, they're actively going through it every day and will do for the rest of their lives (no joke, I know a lady in her 80s, who lost her first husband at 18 and still feels sad about him despite now being two-times widowed).

It would be more helpful if you asked how they're doing rather than making it all about you and how you feel. If there is anything you can help with. Unless you're close, it's unlikely that they will open up or ask for your help, but at least they will feel that they are your focus, not yourself.

And then when you're on your own, please do imagine what you would do, or how would you react to losing your partner. And be honest to yourself. I promise it will put things in a different perspective, and it will make you a more mindful and understanding person when it comes to people experiencing widowhood and loss in general.

11. I DON'T KNOW HOW YOU DO IT

*The manual was automatically delivered
by pigeon-post the day after his death.*

Do you really think they know how they do it? How naive of you.

Realistically, the whole experience is like falling off a boat, not knowing how to swim, and all you can do is to do your best not to drown. Except that instead of a lifeboat saving you, all you have is pieces of rubble to hold onto, and when you eventually reach a stretch of sand, you still need to drag yourself through miles of mud and quicksand to finally reach dry land. All while playing the flute.

What makes the period right after becoming a widow extremely difficult is that they have to be the most vigilant and organized when they are struggling the most. Bureaucracy does not care nor allow mistakes. One wrongly completed form can cause massive issues and nuisances in the future.

You know what question widows often keep asking themselves? *"How am I going to do this?".* They don't know, yet they do it anyway – all of it, powering through every hardship, fighting with every obstacle because it's either this, or giving up. And they know their partner would not want them to give up.

12. You're not alone

You right, my anxiety is constantly keeping me company.

Have you ever heard that you can be very alone, even in a room full of people?

That's how widows feel.

I mean, they are not alone in their situation; there are others out there who lost their partners. They are not alone because they have family, kids or friends around them. That doesn't mean they don't feel alone or isolated.

They do.

Even if they are lucky and have the most supportive family and friends, they have to face this alone. No one can process this for them; no one can face their loss for them, and no one can walk this journey in their shoes but them.

I know that you want to say this to comfort them. To point out all the people who care about them. But they are still missing that one person they need the most, and they need to accept the fact that that person is gone. Your job is not to let them isolate themselves in the process.

13. YOU WILL BE FINE

Maybe, maybe not. One thing for sure:
I will be excellent in pretending to be.

Do you say this to convince them or yourself?

Eventually, yes, they will be 'fine.' Or better. Even happy.
There are two ways to go about this sentence.

The first is the truly helpful one. If you want to ease their
worries about the future and want to convince them that
they will be fine, they will manage – and show that you
will be there to support them along the way.

The second one is quite selfish: it's what you say this to
convince *yourself* that they will be alright, you can just go
on about your life as before, no need to change anything
or offer any additional support (and by support, I don't
mean monetary things; emotional and moral support are
far more helpful to someone who is grieving).

It's quite simple, really. If you want to say it for the first
reason, please do. You only need to remember not to
sound like you trivialize their loss.

On the other hand, if you want to say this for your own
peace of mind, don't. Smile and go away - if you're not
there for them at their hardest, then I'm sorry to be blunt,
but they don't need you.

14. YOU'RE YOUNG,
YOU CAN FIND LOVE AGAIN

I can't even find my glasses when they are on my head, so unless Love decides to knock on my front door, I'm doomed.

It's maybe the most paradoxical thing for a young widow that while everyone tends to assure them that they can and will find love again – they are mercilessly judged when they do.

Then, there is the assumption that they even want to find someone else. Although many widows will open up and look for a new romantic (or physical) relationship, it's also not uncommon for them to remain solo – either by choice or just not being lucky enough to find the One – twice.

Either way, being widowed young is cutting their life in half. If they are in their 20s, then grief will taint the best years of their youth. If it happens in their 30s, especially late 30s, then it's very likely that they won't have any more kids – or if they do, then that clock is ticking, potentially creating a double pressure on the widow. Wanting to grieve "properly" and finding a new person to have children with at the same time. In their early 40s, the thought of going out and finding love (which can be a journey full of disappointment and broken hopes) can be further more daunting.

So, indeed, hypothetically, they can find love, but even if they desperately want it, there are no guarantees whatsoever that they will.

15. ONE DAY YOU WILL FIND SOMEONE TO MAKE YOU HAPPY

Already found him. It's the delivery guy.

It might be a controversial opinion of mine, but having a partner does not necessarily equal happiness and it is possible to be happy and content without one. Obviously, each person is different, and some tolerate solitude more than others.

One thing I'm certain of is that being happy and for that happiness not being dependent on another person, is a goal that not only widows but everyone should aspire to achieve.

There is no need for you to make their future happiness subject to finding a person whether it is a friend or a romantic partner, a therapist, whoever.

What you should say instead is: "*One day, you will be happy again*". Once they are able to find it in themselves, they will be able to fully embrace being happy with someone else.

In the meantime, you can offer a large tub of their favorite ice cream as an acceptable substitute.

16. THEY WOULD WANT YOU TO BE HAPPY

That's some revolutionary information, thank you.

Dealing with loss is very, very hard. They are well aware that their loved one would want them to be happy, and they are not actively choosing to be unhappy; it just happens. And when they are feeling good or have a laugh, they can feel terribly guilty (Like feeling horrible for days after laughing out loud at an old comedy).

There is this pressure a lot of widows put on themselves that they need to grieve *the right way* (whatever that is), and that doesn't allow them to be happy, laugh or just feel good in general. So logically, this sentence should be okay, right? It's not the worst thing to say, but it's not the greatest either.

Instead, you should say: "*You are allowed to be happy*" or "*It's okay to laugh*". Because they are, and it's okay, and neither you nor anyone else should judge them for it.

Them feeling good for a few minutes or hours doesn't mean they won't possibly cry through the night, but validating that they can and should have those smiles will take their self-imposed guilt away. Eventually, there will be more smiles than tears and the pain will lessen. Never fully going away, but moving to the background. And they will be happy – or happier at least.

17. LIFE GOES ON, YOU MUST GO ON WITH IT

Life is a rollercoaster and I have horrible vertigo.

Life goes on. You are right about that. You are right about encouraging them to live their lives – after all, they are not the ones who are gone. And truly, they do go on; they physically can't stop in time and space.

They do go on. Do you mean they don't do it the way you want them to? They don't just continue their lives the way they were? Well, they will never be able to do that because that life is gone.

Their future was reshaped; their present was reset, and every aspect of their lives must be altered to this new reality. And they go on with it – in their own way, often desperately trying to hold onto routines and snippets of normality from their old lives.

Dispute their fears and worries as they go on because they have no option not to. But it's their decision how.

18. BE GRATEFUL FOR THE TIME YOU HAD

My promise was to annoy him for 35 years.
He owes me 30.

Being devastated by not having more time together doesn't mean that they are not grateful for the time they had. There is no minimum time spent together that would qualify as *"sure; we had a good one; I'm not going to miss him / her"*. Losing a partner after 1, 15, or 50 years is equally painful. Trust me, they all will say it was too early for death to do them apart – maybe the reasons will differ.

For someone who got widowed after a short marriage or relationship (also define short), they will cherish the time they had but will long for the future they didn't.

For someone who lost their love after decades together, while they, of course, will be grateful for the years – they will also long for more because being without them can feel too much to bear.

Neither you nor anyone has the right to imply ungratefulness when someone naturally wishes if they could have had more time together. A year. A day. A minute more. It is possible to feel grateful and grieve their time together at the same time.

19. At least you don't have to take care of them anymore.

Do you think I could sell his remaining pills for some pocket change?

Caring for a loved one, seeing them fighting and losing their battle, is exhausting and devastating, especially if they know what the end will be. When hope is gone, all they have is to try and make the last months or weeks bearable and to fill them with memories that can, maybe, overshadow the memories of pain and suffering. It's hard work. Mentally, emotionally, and physically.

This comment indicates that not having to take care of them anymore is a good thing, something they should be happy for. But… they lost their person… under normal circumstances, there is no reason to be happy about that. When it's over, it is absolutely normal for them to feel a little relief. Relief that their loved one doesn't suffer anymore, relief that they don't have to endure their suffering anymore either. Do you know what goes hand in hand with this relief?

Guilt.

You should help them rediscover themselves without belittling their loss.

20. YOU NEED TO LET IT GO

Last time I checked I was not some icy Disney princess.

They do not need to let it go. By the way, what exactly should they let go?

The loss? – that's permanent.

The pain? – only time can ease that.

The memories? – they will **never** let those go.

The whole experience of widowhood? – that is now part of who they are, and they will likely never be the same person they were before.

They can't just *let it go,* even if they want to. You would only say this if you are lucky enough to have never experienced such loss before. And that's great for you. I know you (hopefully) don't say this with malicious intent. You just want them to be better, and letting it go would do that. It wouldn't because the twisted truth is that once they start to move on and *let it go,* the guilt from it can hit them like a ton of bricks.

Grief is a process, and it takes time. Let them take their time.

II.

Eye-rolls,

a.k.a.
please, for the love of God,
think before you speak.

21. BUT YOU ARE TOO YOUNG TO BE A WIDOW!

Well, we are petitioning for the minimum age to be raised to 85, but neither God all Mighty nor the Matrix developers got back to us on that yet.

This is my personal favorite, and I would love to have a tenner for every time someone says this to me.

I get it. When someone hears the word 'widow', they picture an old lady in a cardigan sipping tea on a porch. They don't imagine someone in their early 30s (and I am not even that young; people get widowed at any age from eighteen to eighty and above).

Being a widow is hard at any age. For those who are considered young, it is hard in a different way. They didn't lose someone who was by their side for 30-40 years. They lost something else: their future. They have one; of course, they are not the ones who died, but this future is not the one they imagined. They were stripped of the one they were supposed to have. Together. Life together, (more) kids, holidays, and growing old with one another. And this grief is different. Like a second death, a second grieving process.

Please don't say this – you cannot be more shocked that they are widowed at their age than they are.

22. IT COULD BE WORSE

Thanks for the reminder.
Should I dance the can-can or the chicken dance?

This is probably the most unnecessary nonsense you can say, especially if you add examples of how.

Of course, any and all situation could be worse. They died. I could have died, too. Or the kids. Or the house could have burned down. Or we all could live in a war zone. The fact that it could be worse doesn't make their current situation any better.

Being upset about this comment doesn't mean that they don't appreciate the support or stability they might have. They are upset because this sentence belittles their pain and makes it look like you don't think it's legitimate (enough).

Instead of saying it **could** be worse, tell them that it **will** be better. Just a little bit every day, but nobody says you can't go far with baby steps.

23. DIAMONDS ARE FORMED UNDER PRESSURE.

If it goes on like this, I will turn into the Koh-i-Noor.

You say this to reassure them that they will prevail and come out of the darkness being stronger than ever. Unfortunately, that's not always the case.

They do not want to become a diamond. They don't want to be hardened – not like it doesn't happen anyway. Saying things like this (or the other old-as-time cliché: *what doesn't kill us, makes us stronger*) just indicates that they are just expected to deal with this strongly and bravely and power through, never breaking down.

And for a while, they can and they will. But as time passes – let it be weeks, months, or even years – this will take a toll. Instead of diamonds, the pressure will might as well turn them into a wreck or create such a hard shell around them that anyone trying to get through to them will need a sledge hammer. Pressure is not a good thing, especially because widows put so much on themselves on the top of what life gave them.

Rather than justifying it, ask them how you can help to take some of that pressure off them. They will be grateful.

24. GOD DOESN'T GIVE US MORE
THAN WE CAN HANDLE

I don't even believe in the man,
I shouldn't even be in his database!

This is the religious version of the previous comment. Similarly to other religious comments described in prior pages, this could only soothe those who actually believe in some God, so unless you know that the person is actually religious, simply just don't say this. They are not able to associate with it, nor will they find comfort in them.

Even religious people could find this upsetting. Were they struck with this immersed loss because they could handle it? What is this, some twisted test? Some punishment they somehow deserved? It takes very strong faith not to question their God, who just took away their partner.

If you would like to stick with the theme, you should assure them that God will help them through this hardship and you can cite comforting or relating lines of their sacred scripture.

25. YOU'RE SO YOUNG,
YOU CAN HAVE (MORE) KIDS

Sure, how good are you with superglue and ashes?

Why is it, in general, that if someone who doesn't have kids is constantly being told they should have one, then, when they have one, they are almost immediately pestered about having the next?

First of all, it's basic etiquette that you shouldn't ask questions about this topic from anyone in general because you don't know what their reason is for being childfree / only having one, two, etc.

Secondly, with widows, you can have an educated guess of why they have the number of kids they do, and finding a new person just to have more kids quickly is probably way down low on their to-do list. Some people are ready for a new relationship and even kids sooner than others. Some would be open, but by the time they are ready, their age prevents them. Or their finances. Or whatever. One thing is for sure: you will upset them. Maybe they only ever wanted one and their partner wanted more, and so then the wanted two *with him / her*. Not with some random person they haven't even met yet. It is absolutely possible that someone wanted a (big) family - with *their person*. Who died. And now you just reminded them of a dream they will never have, so you can't really be surprised when they get upset.

26. AREN'T YOU LONELY?

Well, I have a dog to feel needed, a cat to feel ignored and a rabbit to… Ehm… Anyway, I'm good.

Of course, they are lonely! What a question. And there are multiple reasons why they are still alone.

1. They are not ready. Yes, they are lonely but only longing for the company of the one they cannot have anymore.

2. They are ready(ish) but scared. Scared of the whole process of meeting someone, scared of being hurt, scared what everyone else will say or think, scared that in some way they are "cheating".

3. They are perfectly content on their own or have made a decision not to date or look for another partner for whatever reason.

Will day be lonely at days? Of course, they will be. Do you need to remind them? Of course not.

They might want to describe their loneliness to you. If they wanted to do that, you wouldn't have had to ask because they would have brought it up. Where would this conversation even go at all?

"Aren't you lonely? – Yes, I am". Then, there is awkward silence, or worse, relationship advice and other comments you'll find in this book (that you shouldn't say either).

27. YOU NEED SOMEONE TO PROTECT YOU

The heavier you are, the harder it is to kidnap you.
I'm safe enough.

Some comments are usually exclusively said either to widows or widowers. This one is generally told to women – the weaker sex, that needs protection. No comment.

If you want them to be safe, recommend a good alarm system. Or self-defense classes. A smartwatch with an SOS function. So many other options.

Let's say they get into another relationship so they are not alone and safe. How can they know that that new person is safe? That he won't abuse them? How can you?

Sure, (unfortunately) there are many life situations when the presence of a man makes a difference, like going to a mechanic or when speaking to a handyman (respect to those who don't treat women as idiots, but sadly, there are a lot of bad apples out there who would take advantage and if nothing else, charge double).

Do you want to help her to get through these encounters safely? Easy. Do you happen to be a man? Or have a brother/boyfriend/husband who you can spare for an hour to help your friend? Sorted.

28. You need someone to take care of you

I am quite competent as it is, my washer-dryer came with a user manual and I can make beans on toast. Will manage.

Contrary to the previous one, this is mainly said to widowers. And it implies two things. Firstly, that a man must be incompetent in taking care of himself and the household on his own, and secondly, that the sole purpose of having his wife around was taking care of him. Both are wrong and insulting. Of course, every family dynamic is different, and indeed, in a lot of marriages with traditional gender roles, men tend to be less familiar with housework, but this doesn't mean that they are unable to learn it. To suggest getting another partner just to take care of them implies that you think they can't learn or adapt and it's frankly degrading for that future someone as well. Do you want them to have a partner or a maid/cook/babysitter?

Despite old beliefs, cooking and chores are basic skills that everybody should be able to do. They might never have learned these, and now they don't have the person who used to do it all. If you see them struggling with anything from basic household chores to making elaborate hairstyles for their daughter, help them learn how to do it themselves. Letting them weaponize their incompetence or justifying it won't help them. Showing them, like sending easy recipes and videos for easy but cute hairstyles, will do.

29. AT LEAST THEY DIDN'T JUST LEAVE YOU

Like that was ever an option for him. You're cute.

What should they answer for this? Yeey? Thanks?

This whole comment is so hypothetical and it actually implies that a breakup with their significant other somehow would have been worse than them dying.

Sure, breakups are difficult and painful but there is no comparison between them. This implies that widows should be grateful to experience their current heartbreak, not the one of breakups. Really?

If their person had just left them, at least they could have been angry at them. With them dying, the anger they feel is just there without a rightful recipient, a devastating rage inside them against faith, God, the universe...

So, bringing something hypothetical like this is simply unnecessary. The best-case scenario, they will just roll their eyes at you; worst case, they will start making up "what if" scenarios in their mind about something that may or may not ever have happened and you'll make their already tired mind run extra circles it shouldn't.

30. AT LEAST YOU HAD KIDS

What would you say, if your child looked at the sky and said:
"If Daddy is up there, why can't I see him?"
I didn't know either.

Losing the love of your life is only the second worst feeling you experience as a widow. The worst is seeing your child(ren) grieving their parent – regardless of the child's age.

For parents with young kids, it is the constant worry of how to explain it; how to let them know they were so loved by the other parent when they maybe won't even remember him/her? With kids who have memories with their deceased mum or dad, how to help them? How to ease their grief and pain? There is nothing worse than seeing your child suffer without being able to stop it.

Of course, they are grateful for their children, and having them fires their fight to get going – but it is not an easy road. They make every decision, face every trouble, illness, and question on their own, all while being stigmatized as single parents (especially mothers) – after all, it's not on their foreheads that they are widows, and let's be real: people judge.

At least they have kids, yes. But never think that makes it easier, because it's everything but easy. At least they have kids, yes, so all of it is worth it.

31. AT LEAST YOU DIDN'T HAVE KIDS

Yeah, it's a pity.
I'm missing out on quite a lot of tax benefits because of it.

This is one of the cruelest things you can say.

They very likely would sell their souls to the devil himself to have a child with their lost loved one.

A piece of them. Someone to live for.

By the way, do you even know why they didn't have children? Maybe they didn't have the time yet; it was too early - they will always mourn the chance they never had. Perhaps they were waiting to be in a more stable situation – in this case, I assure you that they are banging their heads against the wall because they waited. Maybe they had fertility struggles – then they were already devastated but hopeful, and now that hope is gone as well. Maybe they were never in the right situation, and they are not in one that would be right with a child either and technically you're right – that makes them neither happy nor relieved.

If they didn't have kids, then don't mention kids. Under no circumstances will you be able to comfort them with this.

32. AT LEAST NOW YOU CAN DO AS YOU PLEASE

Indeed, it will be nice to do things without filling out the request form and waiting 3-5 working days for his approval.

Do you know how complicated and bureaucratic it is to lose a spouse? They are not even free to get a nervous breakdown as they please because they are just too busy!

Of course, every marriage dynamic is different, but usually in healthy relationships, both parties can make their own choices. Surely, they probably will discuss things or inform one another and make big decisions together, but generally speaking, they are free to do as they please.

Furthermore, being ~~single~~ alone doesn't automatically mean bigger freedom. Obviously, there is no one to 'report to', but they face different interfering factors, like budgeting issues, childcare, even free time.

No need to glorify or idolize their situation because it's everything but.

And even if we assume that their relationship was controlling on some level and indeed they can now do things that they couldn't do before – it will take time for them to see this as a sort of silver lining. They will, eventually, you just need to be patient with them until they get to that point in their grief journey instead of portraying the loss as a positive thing.

33. AT LEAST NOW YOU ARE FREE TO TRAVEL, GO OUT, HAVE BOBBIES, ETC.

Just to clarify it again, I wasn't held hostage in the basement beforehand, either.

Especially if they've been with their partner for a long time, they have to relearn to live without them. This can include changing how they do certain things they've used to do together, whether traveling, a hobby, or their general home-time routine. Becoming a widow doesn't automatically make any of these easier; quite the opposite, actually.

Just think about it. Although they are theoretically free to do whatever they want, in reality, that's often far from the truth. Hobbies, trips or nights out require funds and time they may not have right now.

Of course, you've said this to cheer them up and to show them that there are things to do, see and experience out there. I get it. But it's scary. It's hard, and not only emotionally. It can be harder financially, even logistically, to travel, go out or just live their everyday life without their partner, especially for those who have kids.

This comment implies that their situation is worthy of envy – trust me there is not a single thing that you would want to envy from a widow.

34. TRAVELING ALONE IS SO BRAVE, I COULDN'T DO IT

*Well, it's either this,
or my couch and the Discovery Channel, so...*

Solo traveling is one of those things that comes naturally to some while simultaneously being other people's nightmare. If they were a solo traveler type before, it would be relatively easy to do it again, either solo or alone with any kids they might have.

On the contrary, many widows have never gone anywhere on their own or as solo parents before. And for them, it's daunting. So I wholeheartedly agree with the first part of this comment. They are brave. The problem is with the second half. Because they thought they couldn't do it either, yet do it anyway. They have no choice. I mean, technically, they do, because they can choose never to go anywhere, and then it's sorted, but would that be a real solution?

Luckily, this is a perfect opportunity for you to both help and empower the widow in your life. Help, because they might need advice and guidance when organizing a trip. Empower, because you can assure them how proud you are that they are doing this. Tell them how proud they should be that they overcome yet another challenge of this new, solo life.

35. YOU SHOULD GET A
<INSERT ANY PET HERE>
(OR WORSE, *GETTING* THEM A PET)

I don't know, his clothes might be too big for a poodle.

You don't want them to be alone. It seems easy to recommend a pet, right? Pets are great. They are. Do you know what else are they? Responsibilities. Expenses. Time. Effort. Things that a widow might can't spare right now.

Being a pet owner is a big task for anyone if they want to do it right. It may not be the best timing to take on another living creature to be responsible for when they are barely able to take care of themselves and their family.

If they want a pet, they will get one. If they are hesitant, you're more than welcomed to encourage them – but only if you think they can do it. Nothing worse than realizing that it doesn't work and then they won't just lose something again – they will feel like a failure for doing so.

There is no quick fix for grief. Not even with the cutest puppy. Once they are ready, they can make a world of difference. It's just all about timing.

36. I KNOW HOW IT IS TO BE A SINGLE PARENT

Your ex-husband still attends every soccer match your son plays.
Not exactly the same, Janet.

This is one of the few comments in this book that can be either perfectly fine or a big no-no, depending on *your* situation. Similarly, when people compare widowhood to divorce (I will get to that on another page), individual circumstances matter.

There are many one-parent families where the other parent is absent for whatever reason. In my opinion, those single parents have the right to compare themselves to widowed parents, as they face very similar everyday challenges.

Single parents who more or less successfully co-parent, however, don't. They don't know how it feels when there is no one to turn to with significant decisions regarding your child. They don't know the heartache when you have to find answers regarding their deceased or absent parent when you don't have any. They don't know the worry that solo parents feel about themselves and the future of their child(ren) God forbid anything would happen to them.

So, if you're group A, you're good to go. Group B, sit down, be quiet, and be grateful. You might be single but your child still has both parents in their lives.

37. I HAVE A FRIEND WHO IS ALSO SINGLE

I'm not a 'single'. I'm a full album.

Technically, you're right. At the same time, you're very, very wrong. Yes, widows are 'single' – in a way – a very different way.

'Regular' single people are alone because it was either their choice or someone else's, or they are just unlucky in love, and their charming prince or princess on the white horse has not arrived yet. A widow being alone was nobody's choice. It was an accident, a tragedy, unplanned and devastating.

They often don't think the same way about dating as other singles. Their heart is not 100% free to take because a part of it will always love their deceased partner, and any future ones need to accept this. It's a package deal that sadly limits their options because, for some reason, way too many people are jealous of this love and expect them to erase it. Sometimes, even the word widow will scare people away.

So yes, they are single, and many of them would love to love and be loved again. It's just a little different. Just like an apple is a fruit and a pineapple is a fruit, there are similarities but they are very different at the same time.

38. WE DIDN'T INVITE YOU SO YOU DON'T FEEL LIKE THE ODD ONE OUT

How thoughtful of you to rub it in.

Okay, so here is the thing. It doesn't matter if you excluded them because you were genuinely conscious that they would be triggered and feel bad in the company of couples or you were worried for yourself that it will be awkward to have them solo among all the lovebirds. The result is the same – they will be offended. You can make the matter worse if they only hear about it afterward, and then you pull this excuse out of your hat.

Even assuming that you had everyone's best interest at heart, this is not the right way to go about it. It's pretty common for people's social circle to shrink after they get widowed. People change, priorities change, and friendships change – especially if they were friends as a couple before. And that's all okay. Nevertheless, this separation still can be cordial and not hurtful.

On the other hand, if you truly care about the widow and don't want to lose them as a friend, in a social gathering scenario the best is to ask them how they feel about attending – how the rest of the group feels. Communication is the best weapon against awkwardness. They are solo, that doesn't mean they have to be an outcast as well.

39. OTHERS HAVE IT WORSE / IT CAN'T BE THAT BAD

…and others have it better. Like a husband who's actually alive.

Contrary to popular belief, others having it worse won't make anyone happier (any decent person anyway). Every man must carry their own cross, and each is just as heavy as any other.

One thing is for sure: Only they can feel its real weight. Sure, you can think they could or should manage differently, even better – why would you think that? You think you could? Conveniently enough, you don't have to.

And right. Some widows have it easier than others, for whatever reason. It could be that they have supportive family around them while others don't, or that they are financially stable where others are not. That is a silver lining that doesn't lessen their loss, doesn't make their pain go away and doesn't make they lives magically great and happy still – only because they are in a slightly better ship in the biggest storm of their lives.

I can't see any other reason for saying these things than trying to make the widow to feel ungrateful for feeling bad, when they have every right to feel as miserable as they want.

40. WAS HE/SHE VACCINATED[1]?

*Yes, he got both: the first with the chip,
and then the second one with the spare batteries as well.*

You can believe in whatever conspiracy theory you please; that's your own prerogative, but do not push that on anyone. First of all, it might have happened before the pandemic and the renaissance of the pro-vax vs. anti-vax argument.

Yes, you are right; every single vaccinated person will die.

So will every non-vaccinated person because we all die at some point. And regardless how firmly you believe in your truth, this is an insensitive question, especially if you don't know how they died. (e.g., it's quite unlikely that someone died in a car crash because they were vaccinated). Not only is insensitive, it's quite intrusive as well - you don't have the right to know the deceased's medical history just so you can justify your beliefs.

---

[1] Disclaimer: the author is pro-vax and believes in modern medical science. That's being said, she accepts different beliefs – until they don't manifest as ignorant and hurtful comments.

41. BE POSITIVE

The only positive element in me is my blood type.

Look, we all got the memo about the importance of positive thinking, that in this way, we can attract all the positive things from the universe, yada-yada.

Not everyone is a glass-half-full type of person to begin with. If we add that trauma and loss can turn the most upbeat people into a defeated and bitter mess, it's not hard to imagine how those who were already not so positive to begin will end up. Hint: rarely more positive.

Telling a grieving person to be more positive is probably as good an idea as telling a screaming person to calm down. It will very likely make them more upset. A positive outlook on life is great, but it's not something you can force or have on command. Some people prefer to be rational, cynical, or even pessimistic, depending on their life experiences. And that's okay.

This being said, there is a difference between not being positive and being depressed – which is understandably quite common for widows to be. If you're worried for them, you can show them the positive side of life so they can see it and experience it themselves. And they still could end up being not so positive overall.

III.

Nosiness,

If it would be your business,
you'd know it already.

42. How did they die?

If you were close enough, you would know. If you don't know, that means you have no business knowing. This is a very uncomfortable question and for what? To satisfy your curiosity?

It could have been an illness – do you expect them to describe their weeks/months/years-long struggle? The pain of seeing them fade away?

It could have been an accident. Do you want to hear about their fatal injuries in graphic detail?

It could have been suicide. Do you really want them to share it when it is still (wrongly) heavily stigmatized?

It could have been one of the 'basics,' a heart attack or a stroke. Oh, do you know someone who dies that way, too?

You just put the widow(er) in an impossible situation, because unless they are confident enough to tell you that it's none of your business, they will share it. The conversation will spiral, and they will end up sharing things they did not want to, but were bullied into sharing.

Don't be a snooper; forget this question.

43. HOW OLD WERE THEY?

6, but in dog years.

Now, you can think that this is a harmless question and many widows will have no problem answering it.

At the same time, this is one of the questions I hate most. It's nosy, and the type that coerces an answer. Even if they are not comfortable disclosing it, they will because their silence would be taken as an indication that their age is something shameful, like too old or young for the widow.

Why is it relevant anyway? Their age has does not affect the widow's loss or grief. It only has to do with your perception and shock level. Were they young? - Oh, that's horrific. Old? - They lived a nice life. There are always comments afterwards, and there is no way they are helpful.

If you are so curious, go and look up the death notices online. The age is usually disclosed there.

44. And There Were No Signs?

Well, to tell the truth, my fortune teller was trying to warn us,
but we decided to stick to essential oils.

There are many instances when there are no signs whatsoever.

Or there were, but at the time, they didn't realize that these are signs or red flags. Trust me, they are searching for these, even if there wasn't any and blaming themselves for not seeing them – even if they could not possibly have known.

Maybe they knew, but it was an aggressive and fast illness.

Just like I said at the nosy question about the cause of death – if you'd be close enough to them, you'd know already. If you don't, this means that you have no business knowing it.

Sure, curiosity is part of human nature, but with these questions, think about what your next question will be. They answer something. Ok. Now you know. So, what did you gain with the information? Is it worth it to upset them and potentially trigger them? There you go. You can be supportive and show compassion without knowing every detail.

45. DID THEY HAVE LIFE INSURANCE?

Oh, sure, I'm thinking of buying an island.
A kitchen island, but still.

What is it with people needing to peep into other people's pockets? Unless you were a beneficiary (in which case you would already know about it), there is no need for you to have this information. Some people are not even comfortable sharing this with family or specifying the amount (if any) for a wide variety of reasons. Following this logic, any potential answer to the usual follow-up question of: *"and what will you be spending it on?"* is also not your concern.

You would need to be very close to the widow to ask this and even then, you shouldn't, but if you do, you shouldn't be offended if they don't answer or don't want to share any details or specifics.

There is only one thing you can tell them when it comes to the topic of life insurance – and even this is only if *they* bring it up – and that is never to give up without a fight. Insurance companies would do anything, lie, cheat, and cross lines so they don't have to pay.

46. AND WHO WILL GET THE INHERITANCE?

Most likely the solicitors given how much they charge.

Inheritance is complicated. Especially when someone dies suddenly and young, they are less likely to have a will and depending on the place they live, widows can get all, half, or even nothing. Regardless, it is usually a long, heartless, and bureaucratic process, during which they are likely to see the worst of some people.

It's frankly exhausting, even when things go smoothly. And when they don't, it can be heartbreaking for them. Estate disputes break families apart, and if the law is not favoring the widow – they can lose even more from their old life. If you're a friend and they know they can trust you, they will talk to you about these.

If you would really like to help or ensure that they get all that they deserve, you can make recommendations. Do you know a good estate lawyer? Pass along the contact details. Are you familiar with local legislation and entitlements? Offer to help them with the bureaucratic nightmare. Do they no know what to do with any potential inheritance? Or the opposite, are they frightened by the debt they inherited? Help them find a good financial advisor.

You don't need to know all the specifics to be helpful.

47. Are you seeing a therapist?

Yepp, Dr. Oetker.

They might go, or not; maybe they tried but didn't help, or they might already have attended even before this happened to them.

While many people are quite open about going to therapy and see it as part of general self-care (as they should), others want to keep it personal for various reasons. Even if you're close to them, if you don't know that they are, indeed, attending therapy – then they either don't or just don't want you to know.

Talking to a professional can be truly helpful, and if you feel that your friend can benefit from therapy, by all means, recommend it to them – but don't be pushy.

Some people need more time to ask for help than others and remember that therapy is not a magic solution that will make their grief go away and make everything the same again. Not to mention that it's not for everyone and it can take time to find a counselor or therapist who works well for them.

Encourage, don't push, and don't ask unless they tell.

48. YOU MUST FIND IT DIFFICULT
WITH THE KID(S)

*I'm already looking into the local convents
to see which one would take her.*

This is more often said to widowers than widows (as if dads would randomly appear from the garage after mum's passing, knowing nothing about their own kids), but of course, not exclusively.

Yes, they probably find it difficult with the kids. Firstly, because they are grieving, too, and for a parent, there is nothing worse than seeing their child in pain, knowing they can do nothing to ease it. They could have a child who's depressed, one who's acting out and a little one who won't even remember the other parent. So yeah, it isn't easy emotionally.

Then there are practical things, like logistics, school runs, other activities and the whole lot which they probably find difficult, too.

So rather than simply pointing out how difficult it must be and commenting on how good/bad they are doing, look for ways to help. Can your kids carpool? Can you offer to babysit one evening so they can do something for themselves? Can you help in any other way? If not, then comments on the topic are worth just as much as Facebook prayers – absolutely nothing.

49. THE LITTLE ONE(S) WON'T REMEMBER HIM/HER ANYWAY

I think he will be the best imaginary friend she will ever have.

One of the most challenging things in being a widow with a young child is to make sure that the kid(s) know who their daddy/mammy was, what they were like, and maybe even get them to love a parent who they don't remember or perhaps never even had the chance to meet.

Now, the widow has the choice to embrace their memory or pretend that the other parent didn't exist. Take down their photos, hide the memories? Or leave them but when the child asks: who is this, just say it doesn't matter. Realistically, even if they never mention their name again, kids are curious and will ask about their other parent eventually.

By talking about them, showing pictures, videos and stories, kids will be able to know who their other parent was. They will even love that parent in their own little way, and it's heartbreakingly beautiful.

Yes, technically, you are right, and there is a chance they won't remember much or at all. Now stop for a second and think before you decide to rub salt into this wound.

50. YOU'RE SPOILING THOSE KIDS BY MOLLYCODDLING THEM THIS MUCH

I can't help it, it's in my job description as a solo mum.

Set one thing straight here: there is a massive difference between creating spoiled, entitled little monsters and giving more attention, cuddles, or leeway to a child who just lost a parent.

They would bring down the stars and the moon for their child if that would to ease their pain. Neither you nor anyone else has the right to judge a widowed parent for using love and care to help their child process their loss, even if you feel that this makes them a weak parent.

Giving them more love, attention, patience, and, sure, even mollycoddling should be normalized – because it is normal. And I tell you something else: this not only feels good for the child, reassuring that their remaining parent is there for them and loves them, but it's good for the parent, too, to have their kids close, to feel that connection, that love – their reason to keep going and fight.

They need all the cuddles and coddles they can get.

51. YOU'RE STILL WEARING YOUR RING? / YOU ALREADY TOOK YOUR RING OFF?

I took it off because some strange little man
with big hairy feet was trying to steal it.

Again, firstly, what is it to you if they wear it or not? It's such an unnecessary judgment. Some people wear it for years or even forever. Some change it over to their other hands. Some wear it on a chain around their neck. People can take it off because they are ready. Others because they are too afraid to lose or damage it. The ring could have become too small or too large with time, or they could have been in an emergency where it had to be cut off.

There can be a million and one reasons why a widow is wearing or not wearing their engagement ring or wedding band. It's a seemingly small thing that, in reality, holds enormous significance and the decision of wearing it or not is a very emotional one and not one to be questioned.

You, by all means, can disagree with or disapprove of their choice, but you never have the right judge them for whatever they choose to do.

52. WILL YOU REMARRY?

If I could tell the future,
I would be focusing on the lottery numbers.

This is such an impossible question – impossible because they cannot possibly answer it. Depending on where they are on their journey, they either cannot even imagine, can imagine but have no idea if it ever happens, or already have decided not to look for a new relationship – but even that is not written in stone.

Opening up to the idea of dating after the losing a spouse is a big thing. Often a scary one. Marrying again can be even bigger as it affects them not just emotionally but likely financially (and not always positively).

If you want to know if they will be ever open to the idea of marrying someone else, ask yourself why do you need to know when they cannot even know it themselves for sure? Unless you are dreaming of marrying them yourself one day, it's not really relevant to you.

They will ask *"Will I?"* from themselves a thousand times, and they will likely make a decision eventually, but despite all this, life might have a different plan for them.

53. YOU CAN'T BE PLANNING TO DIE ALONE

*I'm planning to be a grumpy old cat lady.
I mean the cats might eat me, but I won't be alone.*

The uncomfortable reality is that dying is a lonely thing and a lot of people die with no one but the hospital staff by their side, if that. The moment of death is quite often a lonely one – they can get a fatal heart attack in the room next to you – being alone while you're going about your business at that moment without a clue or sleeping your sweetest dreams.

No one wants or plans to die alone, but some people can be content with the thought and accept that their decision of solitude will likely result in this. Or they are dreading it, but they are just not lucky enough to find a second special person to spend their life with. Neither case warrants your opinion.

You and your nosiness have no right to stir up their worst fears and lowest feelings. If you are worried about them, you can easily ensure that they don't die alone. You know, friends can also visit the hospice to hold their hands.

54. How are you able to stay in this house?

*Camping in the garden
would be quite uncomfortable in this weather.*

It's sad to think about it, but people often die in their own homes. And indeed, many widows can't stand stepping foot in that room again or sitting on that piece of furniture again, and they get rid of it as soon as possible.

But other than a constant reminder, that house, their home, also holds many happy memories. Memories of their life together, and that is more difficult to let go of than a sofa or bed.

Even if they want to, overall, moving is a big thing, a big change and often, they don't need any more changes. Neither do the kids, if there are any.

Realistically, not everyone wants to move. Some people value the home and the idea of '*their home*' enough to tolerate that one devastating memory of finding their loved one or fighting for their lives. Those moments burn into them, and it takes a lot of mental and emotional work to learn to live with them.

Staying in the house is not always a choice. They can have numerous reasons to stay (finances, school, etc.), and if they choose to, then it's not up to you to question that choice.

55. AT LEAST IT'S NICE TO HAVE
A MORTGAGE-FREE HOUSE.

Oh it's easy.
All you need is a husband with a house and good life insurance.
Of course he has to die, but who cares about the little details.

Petty jealousy is a really ugly thing. Being jealous of something that they have because they endured the worst heartbreak of their lives is even worse. Of course, it is a silver lining when they don't have to worry about having a roof over their head.

It's quite common in some countries for banks to request that people take out life insurance that covers their mortgage in case anything happens to them. People can have life insurance through their work as a benefit, or simply being forethoughtful and wanting to ensure their family's stability would the worst happen.

I can assure you that they would exchange the house, life insurance, benefits, pension, whatever they receive to get their partner back in a heartbeat. They can't. So why would you envy this ease in their struggles? Why would you make it as if having a house or money or whatever makes it up for the loss? While it indeed makes it a tad bit easier to go on, it won't change the pain whatsoever.

56. Comments on keeping their belongings

What should I have done? A yard sale after the service?

This is such a personal topic, mainly because the vast majority of widows are planning to keep some of their loved ones' belongings forever.

Some people pack up everything quite quickly because seeing their loved ones' things around would be a constant reminder that they won't come home again. Others don't move a thing for months. There are so many levels to this.

It usually starts with small things – their toiletries, washing that favorite coffee mug they used the last time. Then come the things like work stuff, tools, and things that aren't so personal. Then the clothes, the books, and lastly, the personal items. Some stuff will be thrown out, sold or donated. Some others will be kept in storage for the kids for example.

On average, there is a big-clean up in the first year, but it is completely normal to keep everything as it was for years. Unless you feel that there is an unhealthy obsession with them, just let them be. They are kept because they comfort for the widow and if it's not bothering anyone, they should be just let be.

57. CAN I HAVE HIS/HER XYZ?

Sure, would you like me to throw the car in the bundle, too?

When someone dies, the vultures are always coming.

Of course, it is perfectly normal for family members or close friends to want something meaningful that they can keep, like a piece of clothing or small sentimental objects. This is not about them (although even they should be mindful of the *what* and *when*). I'm talking about people who have no business asking for any of the deceased's belongings.

The opportunists, who think now they can get their hands on tools, cars, jewelry, collectibles, etc. – simply by using the widow's vulnerability.

Is being opportunistic wrong? Yes, in this case, it is. Do you want that X, Y, or Z item so badly? Offer them a fair price for it – *when they are ready to part with it,* and accept 'no' for an answer. They might want to give some things away or sell them anyway, but the transaction should be fair and not coerced. In that way, you created a win-win from a big no-no.

58. BUT THEY PROMISED THAT I CAN HAVE THEIR XYZ

Sure he did.
It must have been a mistake that he willed it to me then.

It's one thing when you ask for something that you'd like, either for free or paid. I went through that on the last page. Coming up with: *"But he prooomiised..."* is just tacky. Do I automatically assume that you're lying? Pardon me if I do.

For two reasons.

One: if they died after a prolonged illness, there were likely discussions about belongings, will, etc., so the widow would know about it already.

Two: if they died suddenly, why would they have promised any of their belongings to anyone? Unless you just agreed to make the deal right before it happened, the widow would quite likely know of any such agreement.

So, assuming that I'm wrong and you aren't just looking for a freebie, timing matters. As they will go through the deceased's belongings and wishes, they will get to you, too. Just don't rush them. Parting with anything can be hard for them. And if they decide not to honor an actually existing promise? (Not the will; that's a legally binding document.) Well, ce la vie… The best course of action is to let it go.

59. YOU STILL CELEBRATE MOTHER'S/FATHER'S DAY?

I'm sorry I didn't get the memo about the rules changing and these holidays are now only being available for the living.

Why wouldn't they?

Many families, especially with older kids, have established routines or traditions for important days like Mother's or Father's Day, birthdays, holidays, etc.. Keeping these traditions or creating new ones while remembering and honoring the parent whom they lost is a beautiful thing.

They might do these for a few years after the loss; they might do it for decades after.

The point is, that it gives comfort not only to the widow but for the whole family and it hurts no one. It brings a broken family together so maybe they can find some peace and heal.

You can find it weird, unnecessary, morbid, whatever… That's your opinion, and maybe it should be kept to yourself this time. A perfect opportunity to apply for the old wisdom: if you have nothing nice to say, don't say anything at all.

60. YOU'RE STILL CELEBRATING HIS/HER BIRTHDAY?

We even threw a birthday party for the cat so what's your point?

Similarly to their decision to celebrate the day of their death, Mother's/Father's day or any important day, why not?

Does it hurt anyone?

Unlikely.

Does it make them feel better to remember their love in whatever way they choose and commemorate the deceased partner (and parent) on their birthday?

Probably, otherwise, they wouldn't do it.

Some people celebrate for a week when it's their own birthday. Others celebrate the birthdays of their pets. Seriously, there are people out there who get excited when it's their favorite celebrity's birthday and they are not judged for it.

So why would you question a widow? Let them celebrate them if they want without judgment and let them let it go if they want without comments. It's their healing process, and if they are not offending or hurting anyone with their decision, you shouldn't offend or hurt them by interrogating them about it.

61. WHEN WILL YOU PUT UP
YOUR CHRISTMAS TREE?

I will use the yucca this year.
A garland, half a dozen baubles and I'm sorted.

All major holidays are quite triggering, especially in the first couple of years after the loss. Christmas can be a particularly difficult period (and don't let me get started on Valentine's Day).

Just think about it. You can't leave the house without seeing families shopping together; partner or family specific presents are in your face on every corner of every store. Presents that they might have bought for their partner.

Actually, you don't even need to leave your home because all you can watch on 90% of commercial television are feelgood family rom-com.

Trigger, trigger, trigger…

… and pressure. Pressure to have a picture perfect, decorated house and to immerse in the holiday spirit.

Well, don't be surprised when the answer to your question is *"I won't this year"* or *"Whenever I have the strength."* For many widows – for a while at least – Christmas and other family-centered holidays are about survival. Getting through them while trying to make it as nice and warm as possible for their kids despite the daunting void they can all feel.

IV.

Self, choices & your subconscious judgements

(and the non-existent appropriate timelines)

62. YOU'VE CHANGED

No kidding, Sherlock,
I wonder why's that.

In the very moment when their partner breathed their last breath everything in their life, present and future, changed. Consequently, they've changed. It was not voluntary, but it was unavoidable. They will keep changing as they find themselves again. It's a process, and in the end, it's still them but another version. One that was formed under pressure and pain and baptized with tears.

I agree that bad habits and constant negative change should be pointed out (mindfully, though). However, they can't really be held accountable for the fact that they've changed. Who wouldn't?

Change can mean anything from hitting rock bottom and staying there to resurrecting like a phoenix, stronger and more resilient than ever – and yes, this includes new habits, new opinions, priorities and even new personality treats.

Frankly, it's quite easy to spiral down when life hits someone hard. Your job is not to blame them for changing but to help them so this change won't go in the wrong direction.

63. YOU USED TO BE FUN

And you used to be skinny but here we are.

There is a saying that people don't change. To some extent, that's true. But there are a number of things that can change people, and tragedies are one of them.

This change is immediate and can be either short-term or permanent. A fun person is often defined as confident, outgoing and open to new experiences or adventures. So for sure, for a period after the loss, widows are not 'fun'. They are distraught, stressed, sad, or even depressed – not fun indeed.

Do you think they want or like it this way? They don't. The good news for them is that they do not need to be 'fun' despite your or anyone else's expectations.

Not now.

Not when avoiding becoming bitter and resentful against the whole world is an everyday struggle.

If you want something fun, do it with someone else. If you can't be even a little understanding of their situation, they need better friends anyway.

64. WHY ARE YOU ALWAYS SO SAD AND NEGATIVE ?

It's just my face now I guess. I think the frown is a refreshing change from my usual resting b*tch face.

If it did not occur to you, they look sad – because they are sad. Frankly, putting on the mask of 'everything is grand' is just too much on some days. Sometimes, they just don't bother to pretend to be fine, so consequently, they can look sad. Or they can show a negative attitude towards things or possibly the whole wide world.

You don't need to be Sherlock Holmes to figure out why they are sad or negative, though. You should be able to make an educated guess. So why would you ask? To hold them culpable, like they are obligated not to show sadness or negativity? It's a shame indeed. They should consider your feelings more and pretend to be alright so you don't feel uncomfortable around them.

Nonetheless, there is a very easy way to turn this around for a more positive result. If you notice that they look or act like they are feeling low, like the universe itself is against them, ask how you can help. Cheer them up! Sometimes a little thing like a joke or a funny video can help – every laugh helps a little.`

65. YOU SHOULD MOVE ON

Okay, bye. What? I'm moving on.

I don't like the expression *moving on*. I prefer *moving forward*. Moving on means that you leave it behind you. I don't think any widow can fully leave the loss behind themselves.

They understand that life goes on, and they will go on with it – but they will carry their loss with them. Their loved ones' memories, their love – and their loss unwillingly formed their identities, and they can't just lock up that chapter of their lives and move on like nothing happened – nor would it be healthy for them to do so.

There are usually two reasons why people say this. One, they care. They don't want to see the widow suffering. Please understand that it's part of the process. Just be there, and they will move forward, slowly but surely. Your only job is to support them on the journey. The second reason is that their grief makes you uncomfortable or awkward, or you're just not happy how the dynamic changed and you want the old them back. That's never going to happen. If you want them to move on for your own interests, for your own comfort, then they, indeed, need to move on.

From you.

66. YOU MOVED ON TOO QUICKLY

Going to the funeral with a new partner is tacky,
anything else is none of your business.

What is 'too quick'? Three months? Six? Three years? Everyone moves forward at different times. Some do so sooner, while some widows may never get into a serious relationship again.

I have to confess that at the beginning I was also judgemental when I was reading about widows meeting new people sooner than what I thought was appropriate. But who am I to judge? Who is anyone? There are just as many reasons why someone would like to start a new chapter than reasons not to.

Especially if you were close to the deceased, you are entitled to your opinion. You can feel hurt by the widow seemingly just moving on without them. But at the same time, they are entitled to live this new life the best they can and to be happy, even if that means seeking a new relationship.

If you are worried that they will be hurt, keep an eye out for them. Make sure that you have their back – there are so many predators out there preying on vulnerable people – and the hardest part is that they often don't see your good intentions. Regardless, they might need you, and when it happens, be there. And if they found happiness again – be happy with them, for them.

67. YOU LOOK GREAT, YOU LOST WEIGHT?

*Yeah, turns out having a crippling pain in my chest 24/7
is much better than cardio.*

It should be basic decency not to comment on someone's weight loss – unless they proudly announce it – because it is not necessarily something they actively worked for. Of course, today's society still holds the view that women need to be skinny and men need to be buff in order to look good and be happy – so complimenting weight loss is seen as an automatic compliment, and I bet nine out of ten women would take it as such. Why do I focus on women? Because weirdly enough, when men suddenly lose significant weigh, people worry about them. Just an interesting double standard here (there will be more).

However, in this case, read the room. What is more logical here? That she hit the gym five times a week and dropped all bad eating habits – or maybe, maybe it's just the stress, the worries and the pain? No meal is tasty with a ball in your throat.

If you notice that your friend is wasting away, take them out for brunch or invite them over for their favorite pot luck dinner.

68. YOU LET YOURSELF GO

*My apologies, looking my best indeed should be
the priority these days, my bad for forgetting it.*

Did they change? Did they gain weight, have their hair in
a messy bun or have a scruffy beard, or not bother with
make-up or nails anymore?

Well, being put together requires a **lot** of effort. The
effort that they don't have when just functioning seems
too much at times. If they have mirrors at home, they
know. And that's one more thing they feel like a failure
for (there are many things that make them feel that way,
even when they are wrong). For you to point it out is
twisting the blade. Especially if you season with:
*"Well, no one will want you if you don't make an effort with your
looks."* – Right now, they don't want anyone else! So
neither a future stranger's, or your opinion matters.
Instead you're more than welcome to keep your
judgmental observations to yourself.

Of course, if neglecting themselves goes on for months
(or years) after bereavement, then you need to intervene
– although, still not with this sentence.

You can help them find their motivation (that is **not**
necessarily a potential new partner). My motivation to
put myself together was not to look like the sloppiest
mum at the playschool. If you know them well enough,
you will find a way to light their spark with time.

69. YOU NEED TO WORK ON YOURSELF
OR YOU WON'T FIND ANYONE

The only person I need to find right now is myself.
Everyone else can wait.

You will achieve exactly two things by saying this. One, they will feel like crap about themselves. They don't look their best; maybe they let themselves go after it happened or maybe there was a little something even beforehand. Insulting is definitely not something their self-esteem needs right now. And two: after the initial shock, they will be insulted. Rightfully so, for multiple reasons. You've implied that they look awful – that's one. Then you've intruded into their personal decisions – how do you know they even want to find anyone? Some widows do; we are not designed to live in solitude, after all. Some, on the other hand, are either not ready (yet) or have made a decision not to. None of those are your business.

While looking good is not their priority, the opposite does affect them (especially women). And I am not saying you can't or shouldn't help them. Looking good feels nice. You just need to find a way to help them in a more subtle way, and without mixing a 'someone' into it – they should look good for themselves. Suggest a spa day or regular runs/walks in the park, and send a link to an (affordable for them) outfit they would look amazing in. Be patient. They will get there.

70. NO FUTURE PARTNER WILL WANT TO SEE THEIR NAME/MEMORY ON YOUR SKIN

It's some numbers and a flower, not a swastika.
Get over it.

Yes, I'm talking about memorial tattoos.

Now, tattoos are not everyone's cup of tea anyway, so why would memorial tattoos be less controversial?

If someone was already into tattoos and even had one or multiple before their loss – they will quite likely get one to honor the memory of their deceased partner.

But the thing with memorial tattoos is that someone who has never had tattoos before, maybe never even considered having one, could just get one, and it would make them happy.

The common thing in all scenarios is that they have their partner in mind – not some future, hypothetical, or potential partner who may or may not like tattoos.

It's their body – their choice, and if anyone has a problem seeing it, well, then they are not the one meant for them.

71. People will not want to compete with a ghost

Rule No. 1:
The use of sage is strictly forbidden throughout the competition.

If they feel the need to compete, they have already lost.

It's that simple. Dating a widow is different, and not everyone is capable of doing it. You see, when a single person or a divorcee enters into a new relationship, their whole heart is open and up for grabs for the new partner.

Widows, however, will always have a reserved place in their hearts that belongs to their deceased partner. This doesn't mean they will not be able to truly love someone else, but they will never stop loving the one they've lost.

Sadly, many people are unable to accept that it is possible to love them both, and in their immaturity, they believe that they need to compete with the deceased memory or 'ghost' or even attempt to erase him/her. If we think about it, this is a great screening measure for any potential romantic partner. If they can't accept and love them with this so-called ghost and fully support the widow however they choose to remember, then they are not fit to become a *Chapter 2*.

72. AT LEAST YOU'VE EXPERIENCED LOVE, SOME PEOPLE NEVER GOT TO HAVE THAT

So?

This comment can have genuinely good intentions to remind the widow how lucky they were to have someone they loved so much in their lives and that the person loved them back 'till their last breath.

On the other hand, it can also come across as plain jealousy. In that case, what would you be jealous of? Their situation? Or just the relationship they had but without the heartbreak because no one would want that, right? If you have any subconscious envy in the back of your mind, let me tell you, this is not the time for it.

This is just another comment that does not help or console them either way. Instead, it implies that they are somehow ungrateful, when they are not. They *are* grateful for every minute they've spent with him/her. Frankly, most widows would willingly choose them again and again even if they knew what they know now. They go to experience it indeed and now they are paying the price, a quite big one I may say. But *at least*, huh?

At this point, I would recommend that if your sentence starts with *"at least,"* just don't even finish it.

73. YOU WON'T ALWAYS THINK OF YOURSELF AS JUST A WIDOW

I think of myself as someone who walked to hell and back.
(and also a widow)

Being a widow is not a scarlet letter. It's not something that needs to be stigmatized. You wouldn't say this to a divorcee, would you? I mean, if they remarry, then that will be their second, third, etc.. marriage. Same for widowers. The only difference is that if someone asks about the first, they have a different answer to give.

They cannot not be a widow anymore. There is always a feeling of belonging when it comes to the late spouse, and that likely remains even if they find love again. That love is partially a result of them being a widow because the person they are now is formed by experiencing all they did, and their new person has fallen in love with this new version of them.

So no, they do not think of themselves as *just a widow*. They think of themselves as someone who walked one of the hardest roads, and it is part of who they are. Of course, not all widows make it such an integral part of their identities – but if they do, then it's a badge of strength.

74. THEY WOULD WANT YOU TO …
<INSERT RANDOM THING HERE>

He told you this? Can I borrow your Ouija board,
mine seem to be broken.

Making decisions, big or small, can be challenging as a widow. First, because they have to make it on their own. Second, because they are afraid they make the wrong one. Third, because whatever they choose to do, someone will judge them for it.

Especially at the beginning of their journey, they will subconsciously lean towards decisions that would align with their loved ones' opinions or would do things their way.

Then, they will start making their own decisions. And unless they want to make an absolutely terrible one that can have a seriously negative effect on their (or their kids, if any) lives, you should only voice your opinion if they ask for it.

Even if they ask you what you think their loved one would have wanted – unless you were their BFF, you shouldn't guess. And you should definitely not use this to influence them into a decision for your sake. This is about them and their journey to find their way forward on their own.

75. HE WOULDN'T LIKE YOU WITH SHORT HAIR
<OR INSERT ANY OTHER DECISION HERE>

If he doesn't like it, he's more than welcomed
to come back and haunt me.

Especially at the beginning, many widows (often subconsciously) make decisions that they would know their deceased partner would agree with. Then there is a first something they just do as they please despite knowing that their partner would disagree with it. Then another, and another and they slowly start to make their own decisions based only on their own stances and this goes way farther than appearance: it can and will be anything and everything.

Making their own decisions – good or bad – enables widows to feel in control at least over certain things. It helps them find the path they want to take in the future because, let's just not forget that they have to re-plan every aspect of their future now. Your job as their friend, family, or acquaintance is to act as their biggest cheerleader and, sure, gently nudge them away from wrong decisions.

So, staying with the original example, unless it really doesn't suit them, just say: hey, love the new style; you're rocking it! (Even if their late partner did not find short hair attractive whatsoever).

76. YOU SHOULD GO OUT MORE OFTEN

Why? I don't like people, all my stuff is at home and I can get plenty of fresh air in the back garden.

Okay, so this comment alone will not achieve much; it's nothing more than a passive suggestion.

It's very true that many widows will recluse themselves at home and subconsciously or even actively avoid people. And you're right. Cocooning themselves in their grief is not healthy. Hence, your recommendation to go out more often seems like a good one. It is, but only if you don't present it with this sentence.

Firstly, depending on the person, when they hear the words 'going out', they think how much it will cost. A movie, dinner, a few drinks, a play – all cost money that they might not have right now. The second thing is they should go out more often, but with who? It should be natural for them to be able to lift up the phone and ask any of their friends, but it's not that easy. Even the best friends don't always know how to interact with widows (hint: should be the same way as before).

So, if you'd like to be helpful, use a more active version of this comment. Say 'W*e should go out,*' and then make plans! Ask them what they want to do (this is good because they can set the budget), and rather than just telling them to go out, take them. Maybe even nag them a little.

77. You Must come!!

Do I have the only sets of keys to the place or what?

Regardless how much you want them to share an important event or celebration with you or you'd just like them to go out for a coffee or something smaller, please accept that *'No'* is a complete sentence.

Going out and facing people can be difficult for widows, especially at the beginning. Scary even, so staying at home often feels safer for them.

Of course, you have the right to feel upset about them not attending whatever big or small event you've invited them to. But I guarantee that you would be upset, too, if they would have a breakdown because something triggered them. You could say that they must learn to handle these triggers. You are right; and they will, but it's not an instant skill.

So when they say no to an invitation, don't push it or try to emotionally blackmail them or make them feel guilty for their decision. Similarly, don't hold it against them if they do end up attending but leave early or abruptly. They probably had their reasons and didn't want to bring attention to themselves.

78. C'MON DON'T BE SAD NOW, IT'S A BIRTHDAY/WHATEVER CELEBRATION!

If I look like I don't want to be here, it's because I don't.

So that day should be a day of celebration, and they are sad? Well, unfortunately, grief is not something that you can just pause for the day. Some days, it can happen. They have an amazing day, no sadness at all, but it doesn't work on command.

Celebrations can be pretty challenging. Birthdays, anniversaries, national or religious holidays – they all can be very triggering to a widow. If they choose to join you, and they try their very best to be there and celebrate with you as best they can, don't pester them to have an ear-to-ear smile.

I know it can bring down the overall mood if someone has a frown on their face. Instead of calling them out, please show compassion, and if you'd like to address it with them, do it privately, away from the crowd. Tell them that you appreciate that they are there, but if they feel it's too much, you won't be upset with them if they leave at any time (there is a good chance they felt obligated to attend).

Celebration days will be easier for them as time passes – but the timeline is different for everyone.

79. IS THAT ANOTHER GLASS OF WINE?

No, it's grape juice.

Everyone copes differently, and some will turn to destructive habits like drinking, smoking, or worse. In today's world, where being a 'wine-mum' is treated as some funny joke and even promoted on social media and in movies, it's hard to judge how much is too much.

You can, and you should worry if your friend or family member turns to something addictive after their loss, if they start chain smoking again, or if instead of numbing their pain, they try to drown it every day. I'm not saying you shouldn't comment on it because it's not something to be ignored – I'm saying that commenting on it won't help. It can even make things worse – like making them do it in secret.

Compassion is key. Patience is key. Awareness is key.

Recognize the signs, be there for them, and make sure you don't judge them. Not everyone is strong by default. Genuine support will do good – judgment without the will to help them could have the opposite result: more guilt, more bad habits, and a downward spiral.

80. YOU'RE BACK TO WORK ALREADY?

*I know, but you see I'm fond of certain luxuries like food
or being able to pay bills.*

Going back to work is a difficult after any traumatic
event. Some people dread it; others find it a much-
needed distraction. In an ideal world, people who
experience loss could return to work whenever they are
ready. Unfortunately, there are these things called living
expenses, and they won't cover themselves.

If you ask this question, it means that, in *your* opinion,
they should have stayed out for longer (doing what, by
the way?). Guess whose opinion was not a factor in their
decision?

If they like their job, being back to a place that is still
normal, and hasn't changed, unlike everything else, can
be really good for them. If they hate their job, then this
is your time to encourage them to change. Even learn
something new if they want and can. Support them to
thrive instead of judging them.

81. GUESS YOU WILL NEED TO GET A JOB NOW

I'm feeling a bit too old to get a sugar daddy, and my lower back is too sore for pole dancing, so I suppose yeah, a job it is.

This trumps the previous question for multiple reasons. If a widow was a stay-at-home wife/husband/partner before, their situation could be extremely fragile, and the thought of joining/returning to the labor market after years (or decades) is very scary.

If they need to, they will, but they dread it because it is very hard to get a job with limited or no experience and a huge gap in the resume with decent wages (not to mention the flexibility to raise children alone). Unless you are prepared to help them in their job hunt, zip it and don't make them even more anxious about it.

Ps.: Helping does not equal getting them a job – that's great, but there are little things you can do: helping with their CV, identifying their strengths, proofreading applications, role-playing for interviews, or lending a suit – just to name a few.

… and be there to cheer them up if they don't get the job and to celebrate when they do.

82. YOU REALLY SHOULD SORT
THEIR HEADSTONE OUT

*I'm on it, but it takes ages to get
the planning permission for the obelisk.*

Okay, so to start with, headstones are a huge decision. First of all, they have to pick something that will commemorate their loved one (and maybe themselves once time has come) for the years, decades, centuries, even; therefore, it has to be the perfect choice, right?

Secondly, headstones (just like anything else death or funeral-related) are expensive. We are talking thousands. That's not something everyone can just flash out right after. Even if they technically could afford it to pay from, for example, the life insurance or some inheritance, going through the probate process can take months, and that's if there are no issues and no one is contesting anything.

And lastly, headstones can represent a form of closure and finalization of something already final. They need to be ready emotionally to make this final step.

The common thread in all of the above is that they might not be comfortable sharing their reasoning with you, but when queried, they will feel obligated to. So then you can judge when you shouldn't.

83. I couldn't keep their ashes in the house / Couldn't part with it

I can't decide if I want to convert his into a diamond.
It's a lot of pressure.

This is a quite sensitive and extremely personal topic: how to say goodbye (or don't) to their remains. Their options differ depending on local customs or legislations – some countries allow the ashes to be shared, scattered, buried, or kept on your fire mantle, while others have strict regulations and demand them to be placed in a cemetery.

Some widows also feel more connected to the remains, while others can easily disconnect and don't see their partner in the pile of ashes. Whichever the case, they've made their decision to suit their emotional needs and not to provoke your judgment. Frankly, unless you are family or a close friend, maybe you shouldn't even mention the ashes at all.

By all means, you have the right to feel uncomfortable with their decision or the presence of an urn, for example, if you visit them often – and you can express this to them as well. This conversation, however, needs to be understanding and free from judgment. We don't have to all agree but we have to respect each other's choices, whether it is based on religion, emotions, or practicality.

V.

The. Worst. Possible. Ones.

(Just stay quiet.)

84. CALL IF YOU NEED ANYTHING [THEN DISAPPEAR INTO THE THIN AIR]

That's nice of you. I'll have your voicemail on speed dial.

Depending on your relationship with the widow, there might be a subconscious expectation that you will be there for them to support them emotionally or in some other capacity.

You can feel pulled in and coerced to help, while feeling that you're unable to do so. You can choose not to without justifying it. Of course, there is a possibility of the relationship being damaged even if you provide reasoning for your absence from the situation, but that's a different conversation.

However.

Do not promise to be there if you can't. It's as simple as that. For the widow, their whole world disappeared from underneath their feet overnight and they need stability. This includes people they can count on. If you are not up to, able, or willing to aid them in the most difficult journey of their lives, then do not fool them with false promises.

This doesn't make you the villain. There can be a hundred reasons why you can't, and that's okay. Just be honest about it with them and with yourself as well.

85. WELL, IT WAS EXPECTED SO YOU SHOULDN'T TAKE IT THIS HARD

Well, we picked an urn that matches the clock on the fire mantle, hopefully that will cheer me up eventually.

Losing someone after a long illness is difficult on another level because their grieving process started earlier, possibly when their partner was still alive. They had to see their partner losing themselves, slowly deteriorating physically, mentally, or both.

They were already grieving the person they used to be – but they were still there; they were still their partner, the father/mother of their child(ren).

With their death, their suffering ended, but the widow's will stay.

No, knowing that this will inevitably happen won't make their grief lessen, nor does it make it easier to process it. They inevitably feel a sort of relief that their love is not suffering anymore. Nevertheless, the loss will still hit them like a ton of bricks because before they woke up every day that, maybe that's the day when they won't have the love of their life anymore and they were given one more day.

Now it's over, and they are gone forever, no more gift of days, just pain.

Don't belittle it.

86. Everyone is experiencing loss at some stage in their lives

*I would have preferred weight loss instead
(and by this I don't mean his 200lbs).*

Franklin said that there are two things in life that are certain: taxes and death.

Now, loss does not necessarily have to mean death. We constantly lose people throughout our lives. Friends, relationships, you name it. Sometimes, we are just drifting away; sometimes, we are betrayed or hurt, and at times, these losses can be difficult.

Albeit, indeed, death is probably the worst of all. And it is a common everyday occurrence.

People die. Others mourn. It's life.

So what? Should the fact that others experienced loss as well, heck, even lost their spouse as well matter in anything?

You can say this with the intention of comforting them – hint: it's not comforting. Or you can say it as a nudge for them to just move on as if nothing special happened. As you might have already figured out, belittling their loss or pain is never a good idea. So, the best way to say this is to not.

87. It's been [X amount of time], you should be over it by now

I'm so sorry, my manual outlining the appropriate timelines was delayed. It wasn't eligible for prime delivery.

First of all, why is it an expectation that they are over it? That's not how loss works. Like how? Should they grieve for X amount of time and then go back to their old lives like nothing happened?

Well guess what? That old life does not exist anymore. Their old self doesn't exist anymore.

They will heal, and they move forward with their life. But they must do so at their own time and pace. As I mentioned so many times before in this book, there is no appropriate time, and it's no one-size-fits-all answer.

Just because you think that enough time passed, they should not feel pressured. There is no rushing in moving forward after a loss. You might not understand this – that's fine, but don't make them feel urged or pressured into acting in a way they are not ready to – purely for your or anyone else's comfort.

88. Referring to them as an 'ex'

When a partner becomes an 'ex', that's a choice. This wasn't.
If it would have been, I'd be serving time right now.

Seriously, an 'ex'? This is hands down one of the worst things you can say to a widow.

Do not say it. Ever.

We did not choose to leave them, and they did not choose to leave us (no, not even if they died by suicide – that still wasn't their choice; it was their mental struggle's doing).

If you insist on expressing the past tense of the relationship, say 'late wife/husband.' Or simply just say wife/husband (unless they remarried) or very simply use their name. You can't go wrong with that one.

89. YOU NEED TO FORGIVE

… is exactly what I'll say to the judge
after I finally lost it on someone from all these comments.

Obviously, there are two different scenarios here. In the first, there is no one to be blamed for the death of their partner. So, whom should they forgive and what?

The other scenario is when there is a person to blame, someone who was responsible beyond doubt. Being able to forgive someone who intentionally or unintentionally took the life of someone they loved so much is not something everyone can do. Frankly, most people would not be able to not hate this person with every fiber of their being.

Yes. Hate is negative energy, and indeed, they could be the bigger person and forgive, but they don't have to. You can't tell them that anyone who is responsible for a lost life deserves forgiveness more than a widow deserves their hate.

If they do find it in their hearts to forgive, it won't happen because you or anyone tells them to. It will only happen if they are ready to let go of the blame, the hate and the surrounding negative energy.

90. Refuse to talk about them or change topic when the widow tries to

You know he just died, right?
He is not an evil wizard whose name you cannot say.

Death can make people feel uncomfortable.

When someone is talking about a lost loved one, one can feel awkward – yet strangely enough, this manifests more often if the loved one who died was a partner. It's less likely that someone changes the topic or judges when the person in question was a parent, another family member, or even a friend.

So why does it have to be awkward when a widow talks/posts/remembers their partner?

I don't have the answer because there is not a single thing that should be awkward or taboo about it. If you have a widow in your life, then you just have to accept that they will not just forget or pretend that their partner didn't exist. They might even talk about them in the present tense and don't add 'late' every time. It's normal, and if this bothers you, then they are not the ones who need to change their attitude.

91. COMPARE IT TO DIVORCE

Well, Karen, your hubby ran off with the babysitter.
That's hardly comparable.

This is a topic that makes 99% of widows enraged. Of course, divorce can be undoubtedly difficult, and there are absolutely horrible divorces with terrible human beings who cause a ton of pain to their ex-partner and often to their children as well. Treason, abandonment, lies, and heartbreak – are all quite common. Despite all of these, a divorce (especially an amicable one) and widowhood are not the same, and they never will be.

I get why one would think that they are similar – because indeed, they have parallels. They are both painful. They both destroy the future one imagined or planned for themselves. They are losses. Divorcees, however, are free to blame, hate or cuss out the leaving partner. They can fight them for their due, they can get justice by the courts or by standing up to them.

Widows can't blame the deceased. Even if they were at fault somehow, they do not want to blame them because that would tarnish their memory. They desperately want to blame someone, and when there is no one to blame, they blame themselves. And this difference alone is enough to enrage widows when someone compares their divorce to their loss.

92. Maybe you just were not meant to be with him

Okey-dokey, nevermind, then.
Brunch anyone?

How exactly should this be comforting? Should the widow just go on about their day like nothing happened, or… ?

This comment can suggest that they picked the wrong one because they picked a person who just died, leaving them behind. Certainly, *The One* wouldn't have done such a thing, right?

No. Of course not.

If we believe in faith and that everything is written in the stars for everyone, then obviously, they weren't '*meant to be*'. Alternatively, life is just unfair. People can lose the love of their lives, the one who they were meant to be with for no reason, and they may or may not be lucky to find true love for a second time.

Regardless of what you think about the compatibility of the widow and their late partner, this is a comment not to be made. They probably weren't perfect (nobody is). They might have had faults. In the shadow of the loss and trauma, the widow will wash these out of their mind, focusing on only the good things. It doesn't matter if they were or were not '*meant to be*'. They chose them, and now they've lost them.

93. YOU WOULD HAVE BEEN
DIVORCED ANYWAY

Still, somehow, alimony has a much nicer sound to it than widow's pension.

Not every relationship is perfect, and no two deaths are the same. In some cases, widows/widowers are less saddened by it than others – for whatever reason. They could have been in an abusive relationship with the deceased, or indeed, they could have contemplated divorce, just to name a few. More often than not, you wouldn't know about their issues, and despite having those issues, they can still be deeply affected by their demise.

Just because you suspect that they had relationship struggles (even if you know it for a fact), you can't automatically assume that those struggles eliminate all grief. They can grieve the time they spent together, the relationship that may or may not have been fixed (and now they will never know), the parent of their children or the chance of having any.

Divorce or separation would have been a *choice*. Their passing was not. In the best case scenario, you will come across as ignorant and hurtful; in the worst case, your comment will be deemed malicious or offensive.

94. YOU SHOULD FIND [INSERT KID(S) NAME HERE] A NEW MUM/DAD

She. Already. Has. A. Father.
And he is still more present than your manners.

There is no such thing as a new mum/dad. They are not lost socks that you can just replace.

Do you mean that they need a second parent? Raising them alone will somehow make them less? Or is the widow a worse parent for doing so? Or do you just think they are incompetent on their own? Maybe it's your family values that dictate that every child should have a mum and a dad. Sure in an ideal world, a child has two parents (not necessarily a mum and a dad but two parents).

Reality is much more complicated. Widowhood is even more, for sure. And even if they enter into a new relationship, that person will never replace the parent who was lost. The memories of that parent, the love and bond they had with the kid(s) is something that need to be respected, remembered for, and cherished.

This doesn't mean that a new person can have the role and love of a parent, but they will be a third one.

Not a replacement one.

95. Offering to 'warm their bed'

I prefer my hot water bottles to be less hairy and more quiet.

Repeat after me:

Widows and widowers. Are. Vulnerable.

Especially at the beginning, loneliness and longing for some sort of intimacy (often as little as a cuddle) can be quite difficult to deal with.

Using and abusing this doesn't mean you are a good friend, or suitor, or simply just opportunistic – it means that you're a predator (regardless of your gender).

Sure, you might be genuinely attracted to the person. That's perfectly fine. Then you need to proceed with even more caution, by giving them time to open up towards you when they are ready. If you genuinely want to be with them, why would you risk them having regrets for jumping too far too soon?

On the other hand, if you are looking for easy fun, I would recommend dating apps instead.

96. I KNOW HOW YOU FEEL.
WHEN MY DOG/GOLDFISH/GERBIL DIED...

?????
(Seriously, this is just so bad,
I can't even think of a cynical remark)

If comparing the loss of a parent/sibling/friend and losing a partner is like comparing apples and pears, then comparing the loss of a pet and the loss of a partner is like comparing apples and lawnmowers.

If losing a pet is the most significant loss you have ever experienced, consider yourself lucky. Sure, pets are family. Pets are a support, even a savior in some cases. That's being said, no, not comparable to the loss of the love of their lives.

This can be extremely upsetting (even insulting) to hear – not only for a widow but anyone who lost a loved one because they feel you just compared their person to an animal. Even if they absolutely adore their pets, I'm sure they would swap Scruffy for their husband/wife in a heartbeat.

Just like many others in the book, another typical example of '*The less you speak, the wiser you are.*'

97. YOU CAN ALWAYS HAVE A NEW PARTNER. I CAN'T HAVE ANOTHER SON/DAUGHTER.

I knew I should have married an orphan with no friends.
Note to self for next time.

Grief can make us selfish. When we lose someone whom we loved dearly, we tend to desperately hold onto anything that belonged to them. This selfishness, this need we feel to keep anything meaningful from them can cause conflict, and it can even turn members of the same family against each other.

Notwithstanding the fact that burying a child is probably the most heartbreaking thing to ever experience, grief is not a competition.

Of course, the widow won't be the only one who has lost the person. They quite likely were a child, a sibling, a cousin, a parent, a friend, a colleague, a mentor, an acquaintance to someone. They all will grieve them, and all of their grieves will be different, but all of their grief will be valid.

Whatever the relationship has been, this is the time to at least respect one another, no matter how painful.

98. TECHNICALLY YOU'RE NOT A WIDOW BECAUSE YOU WERE NOT MARRIED

Thank you, Mr. Grammar Police.
It's really not my fault that there is no word
in the English language to correctly describe me.

This is the wrong time, place, and situation to nitpick over words. They might not have been married. They could have been engaged, living together, only dating… Whichever, they lost their person – the one they loved.

Nowadays, it's fairly common for couples to be together for years or even decades without getting married. They have a family, kids and pets, but having that piece of paper was not essential to them. Does this mean they are somehow entitled to a lesser status or grief? Should they feel less affected or move on any quicker? Do they deserve less compassion because they chose (or simply didn't have the time or chance) to tie the knot?

For them, it's already enough that they are not a widow in the eyes of the law, so they have fewer options and help available – their moral status as widows should not be questioned on top of that. The heartbreak after losing a partner is the same regardless. There is no need to twist that knife with being fixated on the word.

99. Blaming Them[2]

I'm wondering what's bigger right now:
my fear from an assault charge or my urge to hurt you.

Do. Not. Blame. Them. Ever.

They will blame themselves anyway.

They will blame themselves if they were there because they couldn't save them. They will blame themselves if they haven't been there because what if they could have saved them. They will relive every argument and every nasty thing they've ever said, and they will regret an awful number of things.

Are they right to do all of these? Of course not. But they feel they need to blame someone – and even if there is one person to blame, they will reserve some for themselves. It's not healthy, and it takes time and a ton of positive reassurance that they are not to blame.

Even if you were close to the deceased and loved them dearly – don't blame their widow(er) where no blame is justified. It's cruel, and it won't change anything.

---

[2] There are certain, horrible situations when the partner could be at fault, like in a car crash where they were driving. Still, pointing out their blame will not make you happier and won't bring the person back. Living with it is enough punishment for them.

100. THAT'S CRAZY!!!

I kno-ooow [jazz-hands]

It is crazy.

The whole thing, their lives, the motions and emotions, the stress, the tears, the rollercoaster of feelings that are more unpredictable than the Irish weather – *all of it.*

Do they look crazy sometimes? Do they act crazy? By whose standards, by the way? Can you define it? 'Crazy' as in a medical sense or just because you did not expect them to do, say, or react in a particular manner to something or someone?

Most importantly, know that they are doing their very best not to lose their marbles for real and somehow preserve their own sanity in this whole new, upside-down, inside-out world of theirs. This can mean that they are not their usual self; it can even mean the polar opposite.

Crazy? Crazy. So be it.

Made in the USA
Monee, IL
07 July 2026

56549918R00069